Belshazzar and Antigone

By

G. E. Kruckeberg

This book is a work of non-fiction. Names and places have been changed to protect the privacy of all individuals. The events and situations are true.

First published by AuthorHouse 08/10/04

ISBN: 1-4184-9365-1 (e-book)
ISBN: 1-4184-4123-6 (Paperback)

This book is printed on acid-free paper.

This book is dedicated to:

ANNIE

My wife's a perfect lady – lovely as she can be.
I'll never understand just what she sees in me.
I know you'll think I'm crazy; I know this sounds absurd,
But I'm married to the most beautiful woman in the world.

She's every inch a woman; she's very much a child.
She's everything I need to make my world all right.
She's all I've ever wanted and more than I deserve.
I'm married to the most beautiful woman in the world.

FOREWORD

There are many reasons why
People poetry might write
(And many things they could do worse
Than pen a line or two of verse).
Some write poems to make you cry,
Some to make a lover sigh,
Some for money, fame, or pity,
And some to ease indignity.

Some write poems to make you sad;
Others write to make you mad.
Some write to make you laugh or blush,
But most write poems because they must.
Rhyme and meter might enthrall
Those who read his doggerel,
But to the poet, poetry's
A method of discovery.

Poetry's a private thing,
And its writing often brings
A new perspective that will help
The poet understand himself.
Yet no emotion is unique,
And poems oft to all bespeak
The thread of commonality
That binds us in humanity.

Let me therefore offer you
And your progeny a few
Lines of poetry that I've penned
(And that I highly recommend)
In hopes that they'll give you at least
As much as I hope they'll give me.
For, though I wrote them for myself,
I've always hoped that they might sell.

TABLE OF CONTENTS

APPOLOGY

Should my habit of reiterating cogent points offend,
Or if you think too often I repeat a common verity,
These three maxims to your consideration I commend:
Redundancy is the soul of clarity,
Redundancy is the soul of clarity,
And redundancy is the soul of clarity.

BELSHAZZAR AND ANTIGONE

Belshazzar and Antigone,
Two neighborhood felines,
Upon our garden fence did meet
One evening just at nine.
They soon were busily discussing
Feline world affairs,
And from my window up above
I heard them talking there.

"I wish I were an inside pet,"
Antigone meowed.
"I'd never more be cold or wet,
And I would be allowed
To play with pencils on the desk
Or sleep upon the bed,
And when I wanted to, I'd let
My mistress scratch my head."

"You ought not wish for things like that,"
Belshazzar then advised.
"Remember that being a cat
Means being satisfied.
For what is is; what's not is not,
And you should never fret
About the life you haven't got,
'Cause life is what you get."

"At least I'm not a dog like that,"
Antigone then said.
She nodded at our schnauzer napping
In my flower bed.
"How such a stupid animal
Could be a man's best friend
I'll never understand at all."
Belshazzar said, "Amen!"

1

"Dogs just don't know the secrets of
Success," Belshazzar said,
"Like never blink, and never bluff,
And never hesitate.
One must learn, if he would succeed,
The first law of the cat:
'If anything attacks, retreat;
If it retreats, attack.'"

Antigone scratched at a flea
And said, "Not long ago
I chased a butterfly retreating
Through an open window.
I felt like such a fool, although
I landed on my feet."
"Well that was then and this is now,"
Belshazzar said. "Let's eat."

"Montoni's garbage can is near,
And so is Wong's," he purred.
"Italian or Chinese, my dear?
They're both quite good, I've heard."
Antigone said, "This is why
I like being a cat:
We never ask too much of life,
And so we never lack."

Then, in a wink, they both were gone
Across the garden shed,
And in my room I pondered long
Upon the things they'd said.
I've learned to handle joy and strife
From winsome scamps like that,
And much of what I know of life
I learned from watching cats.

CATS

Cats have personalities
(Or personal idiosyncrasies):
Some are mellow and some are mean,
But all of them are neat and clean;
Some are solemn and some are gay,
But they all like to sleep all day;
And whether outside or inside,
They all prefer to roam at night.
Their differences, it seems, are less
Significant than their sameness.
They can be yellow, white, or black,
But every one of them's a cat.

People are a lot like cats
(Though some might disagree with that):
Whether timid or masterly,
They all respond to flattery;
And some love once, some many times,
But each one loves one at a time;
They can be peasants, priests, or kings
But they all laugh at the same things.
The similarities, I guess,
By far outweigh the differences.
Whether we're yellow, white, or tan,
Every one of us is a man.

G. E. Kruckeberg

TWO DOGS

Two dogs one day were walking
When in the park they met,
And they soon fell to talking
About their human pets.
"My people sure are odd," said one,
"Till ten last night they sat
And just stared at television.
Why, they're dumber than the cat."

"That's nothing," said the other,
"My humans stand around
And bark at one another
Like crazy Basset Hounds.
Or else they sit for hours and look,
Like some half-witted pup,
At something that they call a book.
But don't ever chew one up!"

"What gets me," said the first one,
"Is how they're never there.
They jump in their Suburban
And drive away somewhere.
And when they finally do get back,
They don't have time to hear
About the day that I have had,
Or to scratch behind my ears."

"Most humans seem enamored,"
The second dog observed,
"With horribly bad manners,
If that's the proper word.
They conduct themselves so crudely
It almost makes you blush,
And they treat us so rudely
One would think that they owned us."

"My humans lose their temper,"
The first dog said anon.
"You'd think they had distemper,
The way they carry on.
Sometimes they snap and growl like Chows
And yap like Pekinese.
And if I chew inside the house,
They will even snap at me."

"Yes, humans sure are funny,"
The second dog opined.
"There's something they call money
They're after all the time.
It isn't good to eat, of course;
I know, 'cause once I tried.
I don't know what it's good for,
But it keeps them satisfied."

"Well, it's been very pleasant,"
The second dog then said,
"But I must leave at present;
That's my house up ahead."
The first dog said, "I've much enjoyed
Our pleasant little talk,
And 'though with humans you're annoyed,
Just be glad that you're a dog."

BIRDS

Birds are the epitome
Of freedom, and like poetry,
They sore above the spoil and strife
Of our earth-trammeled prison.
They live in the unbounded sky
Between the earth and heaven.

Thus we say, "free as a bird."
From childhood on that phrase we've heard.
And birds *are* free - to be destroyed
By cats and cars and red hawks,
And free to be shot at by boys
With beebee guns and slingshots.

Could it be that being free
Is not all it's cracked up to be?
Do not birds kept in a cage
Live longer than their brothers?
(But do they thus improve the race
Or livelihood of others?)

Freedom is not won by chance
But by eternal vigilance,
And each life lived in freedom makes
A stronger, better breed,
For we're as free to make mistakes
As we are to succeed.

Birds display great staying power -
Descendants of the dinosaurs,
They show us freedom isn't cheap,
But that it has no rival.
It's cost: responsibility;
It's benefit: survival.

CLOUDS

The clouds are paper cutouts
Pasted immovably
Upon the dim horizon out
Beyond a painted sea.
Clouds like a backdrop on a stage
Without a play we see -
Clouds without time or end or age -
A glimpse of eternity.

Clouds are cameos upon
A sky of Wedgwood blue,
Depicting gargoyles, gyrfalcons,
And handsome ladies, too.
Their shifting images inspire
Diligence and patience,
For they ignite the vibrant fire
Of our imaginations.

The clouds are fairy castles
Reaching up to the sky;
From their marble towers tasseled
And wispy banners fly.
But they snow upon the mountains
And shower upon the plain,
And their columns rise in fountains
That can turn to hail the rain.

The steel-wool clouds are fashioned
Like valkyries of old,
And their woolen robes are fastened
By slender lightening bolts.
With the voice of Thor behind them
They stride across the land,
Taking all who would defy them
To Valhalla's misty strand.

G. E. Kruckeberg

A flock of dirty gray sheep
Driven by urgent gusts,
A slowly moving pirate fleet
With sails of cumulus,
Angels, demons, and manatees -
All sculpted by the wind.
Clouds are whate'er in them we see;
They're a mirror of the mind.

THE WIND

It's still as death, and stirs not a breath
In the hour before the dawn;
Then the stars depart and the west wind starts,
To her lover, Phoebus, drawn.
And the first faint breeze in the live oak trees
In a husky whisper speaks
Of love that's lost and of bridges crossed
And of things that ne'er will be.

The wind is soft as a lover's touch
When she's steady in her course,
But she's loud and wild as a restless child
When she's blowing from the north.
Then her cry is spiced with the sting of ice,
And she numbs the naked cheek
And molds the snow into smooth windrows
Over road and fence and creek.

She brings the rain and the hurricane
When she's blowing from the south,
And her voice is keen as a woman's scream
As she howls around the house.
But the leaden sky and the clouds piled high
Make the blood course through your veins,
And gusting air in your dancing hair
Makes you feel alive again.

When day is done and the fading sun
Sets the western sky ablaze,
Then the night wind creeps from the purple east
To caress her lover's face.
And as we reflect and resurrect
All the day's defeats and sorrows,
Her calming breath murmurs promises
Of a better day tomorrow.

G. E. Kruckeberg

SUNRISES AND SUNSETS

A sunset is a splendid thing;
On the inverted bowl
Of heaven, brash Apollo flings
His evanescent coals.
But finer is the blush that springs
Pale Venus to enfold,
And sunrises are better for the soul.

A sunset poets may inspire
Its beauty to extol;
Their words vicariously aspire
To gild its liquid gold.
But it's far better to admire
A sunrise than a scroll,
And sunrises are better for your soul.

The world with endings is concerned
Too often, on the whole;
In each beginning we discern
An ending as its goal.
Yet endings even sundown spurns,
For sunrise is its foal.
And sunrises are better for the soul.

CARPE DIEM

Now in the roseate East
Bright Lucifer proceeds
Apollo's fiery steeds
To Heaven,
And men of toil arise
To pain and compromise
And hate that blinds the eyes
Of reason.

And women comb their hair
And don their cloaks of care
And pray God's aid in their
Endeavors,
While children rise to play,
All unaware that they
Alone will seize this day
Forever.

G. E. Kruckeberg

SEA MOODS

The sea like a woman beckons;
Her arms are the roiling foam,
And the swell of her heaving bosom
Has lured many a man from his home.
She's a beauty to behold,
But the depths of her soul are cold.

The sea is a woman angered,
Hurling herself on the land,
And lashing with fury untrammeled
The pretentious inventions of man.
With the lightning in her hair,
She's a hellion of beauty rare.

The sea is a brazen harlot,
In a gown of sea haze spun,
And her diamond studded tiara
Is ablaze in the afternoon sun.
She's a lovely thing to see,
But her favors are far from free.

The sea is a gracious mistress
Wrapped in the robes of the night,
And the moon on her raven tresses
Glistens silver and amber and white.
She's as gentle as a child,
But her heart is restless and wild.

The sea is a wanton lover,
But the whisper of her breath
On your hot cheek as you embrace her
Has the haunting aroma of death.
For it's equal to the sea
Whether she grave or lover be.

SPRING

The ice is gone
From the lake, and on
The island in its center,
A loan, white patch
On the parchment grass
Is the last vestige of winter.
And black and thick
As the river Styx
Is the water at the shoreline,
With golden specks
In its murky depths,
That reflect the morning sunshine,

The sky's blue bisque,
And the morning mist
The trees from earth dismember.
The old pine tree
Lost its top, I see,
In the sleet storm last December.
The sound of geese
On the warming breeze
Whets our anticipation,
And crocuses
Are preparing buds
For their sudden celebration.

All nature seems
Frozen in a dream,
Awaiting Spring's arrival,
And the mind suspends
Dreary plots and plans
For it's annual revival.
The brave rebirth
Of the gray, old earth
Each year our hearts embolden;
Forget then we
Our mortality
For a brief, exciting moment.

G. E. Kruckeberg

RAIN

There's nothing quite
Like the rattle of rain
On your window pane
In the middle of the night.
It makes you feel warm
And safe from harm,
And its droning refrains
To a peaceful sleep invite.

The rain is sweet
As a lover's caress,
And her windblown tresses
Fall soft against the cheek.
And the slate smooth lake
Is decorated
With diamond impressions
Across its face wind-streaked.

The rain's soft beat
On umbrellas drum-tight
Reverie excites
'Mid the bustle of the street,
And shimmering wet
Pavement reflects
The traffic's bleary lights
And the streetlamps misty-wreathed.

The crystal drops
Are a vital baptism,
And their vibrant rhythm
Brings to life the leaden sod.
The desolate earth
Quenches its thirst
In the rainbow-hued prisms
Of the fountain of the gods.

TREES

Three things a man must need have done
Before his life's complete:
Take a wife and father a son
And plant at least one tree.
And three things are to a man forbade:
Never lie, never cheat, never slack.
And to these three yet another add:
Never take what you can't give back.

John Chapman was a simple man.
With just a sack of seeds,
He wandered over Indiana
Planting apple trees.
The Indians thought he was crazy;
People called him Johnny Appleseed.
They said he was shiftless and lazy -
But he never did kill a tree.

Paul Bunyan was a mighty man;
With double-bitted ax,
He raped the woods of Michigan
And put ne'er one tree back.
We choose our heroes not for their good
But because they are bigger than life,
And it matters not if they make wood
From trees that we need to survive.

Where once stood oaks and pine trees tall,
Now stands a filling station;
And parking lots and shopping malls
Entomb all vegetation.
After eons of evolution,
We have traded survival for greed -
And traded clean air for pollution
By killing off all of the trees.

15

G. E. Kruckeberg

Like druids of old we decry
The cutting down of trees,
For their rich foliage purifies
The very air we breathe.
So plant a tree, both for the living
And for progeny not yet conceived,
For even more blessed than giving
Is giving back what you've received.

AUTUMN

The summer's dying embers
Warm the days of mid-September,
But the promise of November
Whispers in the evening breeze,
And the morning chill excites
Memories of winter nights
And of shadowed, shifting firelight
Glistening bright on Christmas trees.

Autumn is a bullfrog's croak
And the pungent smell of woodsmoke
And the warm caress of old coats,
Cedar-scented and well-worn;
It's the far-off call of geese
And the gold and scarlet leaves
That change the dreary gray-green trees
Into pyres that shame the morn.

Summer's Fall is Winter's Spring.
It's a time to rest from working
And enjoy the earth's disbursing
Of the fruits of Summer's toil -
A time for us to savor
The bounty of our labor
And to give thanks for whatever
Of God's favors we've enjoyed.

NATURE

Nature's a woman of many moods,
And of constantly changing attitudes.
On conflict and caprice she thrives
(But she teaches that strength proceeds from strife).
From studying nature, one concludes
That change is the stuff of life.

The clouds slow dancing across the sky -
The metamorphosis of butterflies -
(The world would be a dreary place
Without the excitement that change conveys).
All things grow and mature and then die,
As we, too, must do one day.

Some say we then to heaven shall go
(If a heaven there be, that may be so),
But I, for one, cannot believe
That heaven earth's beauty could e'er exceed.
For earth is all of heaven I know,
And all the heaven I need.

PRIMARY COLORS

Blue is the color of babys' eyes,
Of wood smoke and oceans and clear summer skies,
Of far-away mountains and quiet streams,
And blue is the color of dreams.

Green is the color of tarnished brass,
Of jade, Christmas holly, and meadows of grass,
Of pine trees that cling to the mountain's slope,
And green is the color of hope.

Red is the color of rubies rare,
Of apples and embers and my true love's hair,
Of valentine roses that girls dream of,
And red is the color of love.

Yellow's the color of mustard seeds,
Of saffron and sunrise and rosary beads,
Of newspaper clippings in bibles saved,
And yellow's the color of faith.

White is the color of bridal gowns,
Of edelweiss, ivory, and soft eiderdown,
Of girls' summer dresses and Sunday shoes,
And white is the color of truth.

Brown is the color of weathered wood,
Of old leather saddles and fatherhood,
Of smooth-handled axes covered with rust,
And brown is the color of trust.

G. E. Kruckeberg

THE HEARTLAND OF AMERICA

From Fort Wayne, Indiana
To Fort Payne, Alabama,
And from sunny Texarkana
To the West Virginia Hills,
There're millions of Americans
Who're proud of their inheritance
And ask only to have the chance
To work and pay their bills.

In towns serene and peaceful,
Enriched with friendly people,
Where it's safe at night, and steeples
Are more numerous than bars,
Live America's heartlanders,
Who read Peanuts and Ann Landers
And think pickup trucks are handier
Than fancy foreign cars.

From the fish of Saginaw
To the rice of Arkansas,
From Ohio's cattle and hogs
To Wisconsin's hearty curds,
From the bounty of their labor
And the grace of God's good favor
And the rich, black earth they savor,
The heartland feeds the world.

From the fields of rippling wheat
And the sun drenched cornrows neat,
From cotton fields and fishing fleets
And from orchards ripe with fruit,
From its plains and quiet waters
Come the heartland's sons and daughters,
As ambitious as their fathers
And honest as their roots.

To the cities' grimy slums
And the bustling factories' hum
Have come waves of generations
Their traditions to impart.
Their hard work and dedication
Are a source of inspiration;
They're the strength of this great nation,
For the heartland's in their hearts.

G. E. Kruckeberg

AN AMERICAN TRAGEDY

At six I'm home and after shuffling
Through the morning's mail,
I head for the recovery room
To build a rusty nail.
The clink of ice my thirsty soul
Revives, and I set out
With drink in hand to find out what
My progeny's about.
I find them in the den, stretched out
In front of the TV.
"Hi, Dad," they say in unison
Without looking at me.

"Hi, guys," I say as I sit down,
Then query, "Where's your Mother?"
Kevin shrugs and Darryl says,
"She went someplace or other."
I watch the John Wayne movie,
Though I've seen it twice before,
And when it's over, my watch says
It's seven-twenty-four.
Then to the kitchen I repair,
Turn on the coffee maker,
And see what there might be to eat
In the refrigerator.

Bologna, cheese, cold chicken, bread,
Ketchup, and luncheon meat
I set out on the table and
Then call the boys to eat.
Two troglodytes with bleary eyes
And obvious apprehensions
Emerge into an unfamiliar
World of three dimensions
Where life is played out in the raw,
Not on a little screen
In neatly packaged segments
With commercials in between.

They blink their eyes and peer at me.
"Oh, hi Dad," Kevin mutters.
"When did you get home?" says Darryl,
"And where's the peanut butter?"
The clock above the kitchen sink
Tells me it's nearly eight.
"I hope your Mom won't mind," I say,
"That we already ate.
I wonder where the heck she is."
"Oh, by the way," says Kevin,
"Mom wants you to pick her up
In front of the church at seven."

G. E. Kruckeberg

JUST RENTING

You love the brand new car you bought,
But by the time it's paid for,
You find the thing is so worn out
A new one you must trade for.
The vicious cycle is unending,
'Cause you're not buying it – you're renting.

The great American dream, they say's,
To spend more than you're making.
The most important thing these days
Is your good credit rating -
And how you can secure more lending.
You never own things – you're just renting.

We all want someplace to call home -
To hold against all claimants.
We work our fingers to the bone
To make the first down payment.
And payments we keep right on sending,
'Cause we don't own it - we're just renting.

And when the last installment's paid,
There still is no relaxing.
The title's yours, but I'm afraid
Four governments keep taxing.
And governments are unrelenting.
You never own it - you're just renting.

Then when at last your kids are grown,
And you've put them through college,
They'll simply go off on their own
And leave you with the mortgage.
For twenty years on them you're spending,
But you don't own them - you were just renting.

And when you're gone and all the frills
You worked so hard at buying
Are trashed or given to Goodwill,
You'll realize that dying's
Just payment of the balance ending.
You never owned life - you were just renting.

G. E. Kruckeberg

THE BOOMERS

I was born in nineteen-thirty-four,
Eight years before the Second World War.
The war was over in 'forty-five,
And all of the men who had survived
Came home, their former lives to resume,
And started what we called the baby boom.

The baby boomers were all the kids
Born from 'forty-six to 'sixty-six -
Seventy million, they estimate
(One every ten seconds for two decades).
They swelled like a demographic tumor,
And we were awash in baby boomers.

No generation in history
Has had more opportunity,
And, though their manners were atrocious,
They were wealthy and precocious.
From early on, we'd heard it rumored:
Success was assured the baby boomers.

We went to Korea, then to college,
While they watched Kukla, Fran, and Ollie;
Then, while we worked to educate them,
They demonstrated against Viet Nam.
It's hard to keep your sense of humor
When you're betrayed by baby boomers.

For most of my life I've watched them grow,
From house apes to yuppies to fifty-year-olds,
And as they grew, at each new stage,
The nation grew their needs to assuage.
They were the ultimate consumers;
Everyone courted the baby boomers.

Tooth toughening tooth paste was conceived
After I'd had twenty cavities;
And when Arm and Hammer was introduced,
Half of my teeth were already loose.
For all my life I've been there sooner,
One step ahead of the baby boomers.

They fought in the sexual revolution,
And they invented the word pollution;
From social activism to sex,
We followed wherever the boomers led.
Sometimes I think I'm just a late bloomer -
One step behind the baby boomers.

INSOMNIA

At half past two I wake up
And can't go back to sleep.
I count backward
From one hundred,
And then try counting sheep.

I listen to the night sounds
And noises houses make,
And suddenly
It's half past three,
And I'm still wide-awake.

The clock out in the hallway
Tells me the hour is four.
I count the times
The damn thing chimes
And toss and turn some more.

At half past four I'm drowsy,
But I'm just dozing when
The neighbor's cat
Gets in a spat
And wakes me up again.

At five I hear the hall clock
And turn off the alarm.
I might as well
Get up, but hell,
The bed feels nice and warm.

And now the hall clock wakes me.
Did it strike eight just then?
The bedside clock
I view with shock.
I've overslept again!

THE BALLAD OF VERNON HOWELL

Vernon Howell took a match
And set fire to his booby hatch.
He said, "I'll show 'em who's insane,"
And put a bullet through his brain.

Vernon Howell had eight wives.
'Told 'em he was Koresh the wise.
They were properly inspired,
Until he set their house on fire.

The NRA was there that day,
Watching Vernon blaze away.
They said, "He's our kind of guy.
Let's blame this on the FBI."

NBC and CBS
Tried to blame the BATF.
ABC said, "Let's be fair.
The National Guard was also there."

The Attorney General, in her turn,
Was blamed for letting Vernon burn.
TBS and CNN
Tried to blame the President.

Vernon's Mama blamed the press
For making Vernon kill himse'f.
His Daddy said, "She may be right.
Vernon never was too bright."

The federal men said they were done,
And they went back to Washington.
The Texas Rangers then were left
The job of cleaning up the mess.

Vernon Howell is dead and gone.
Whether he was right or wrong
No one knows, and if they did,
No one really gives a shit.

THE MONKEY LAW

When Frank White was the governor of
The state of Arkansas,
The preachers got to Little Rock
And passed the Monkey Law.
The Monkey Law said Arkansas
Schools had to teach their kids
Evolution 'cording to some
Book called Genesis.
But some folks saw the Monkey Law
As church hegemony,
And there were some questioned its
Constitutionality.

Then those who thought that freedom ought
To not be sold too short
Took the State and the creationists
To federal court.
They said that Arkansas was part
Of the twentieth century;
The Baptists said that man was made
In four thousand BC.
While they contended weeks on end,
We looked on in dismay.
And Little Rock was the laughing stock
Of the whole dang USA.

The major paper in the state
Was the Arkansas Gazette.
It was anti-black and Democrat
And dry as opposed to wet.
The Arkansas Gazette was all
Behind the Monkey Law;
They said that what was good for God
Was good for Arkansas.
They claimed that some Republican
Had started all the fuss,
But I never saw an Arkansas
Gazette that you could trust.

The ACLU, Jerry Fallwell too,
And even Doctor Spock,
And all their spawn descended on
The town of Little Rock.
And when the dust had cleared and justice
Was restored to all,
The State was ordered by the court
To repeal the Monkey Law.
The moral, I guess, was best expressed
By good old Governor White:
"Don't ever mix your politics
With what you think is right."

THE ALAMO

In eighteen-hundred-and-thirty-six,
Will Travis was sent by Governor Smith
To Bexar, near San Antonio,
And the fortress there called the Alamo.
His orders were simple and direct:
To Colonel Jim Bowie pay his respects,
Then pull the powder and canons back
To fortify Fannin at Goliad.

Bowie thought Texas had won the war;
In December, barely two months before,
Milam attacked San Antonio
And captured the guns of the Alamo.
General Cos gave up the Alamo
And went with his troops back to Mexico.
The Texans' hubris, though, had one flaw:
Cos was Santa Anna's brother-in-law.

Bowie was confident however
That the war with Mexico was over.
His Cajun *elan* could not admit
That they'd the fuse of a powder keg lit.
Whether Travis of that was convinced
Or preferred the Alamo for defense
We never shall know; but this we know:
He agreed to stay in the Alamo.

Now the Napoleon of the West,
Leading an army composed of the best
Troops in the country of Mexico,
Is fording the river at Laredo.
Over the creeks and rivers in flood -
Over the raw earth the color of blood,
Burned bare of grass his horses to slow -
Santa Anna rides to the Alamo.

"'Scout comin' in," the gate picket cried;
Travis and Bowie both hurried outside.
Then through the gate, a rider dashed in
And reined up his pony in front of them.
"Mexican scouts - 'bout three miles away,"
He said with a curse, "and headin' this way."
"Bring in the other scouts," Travis said,
"Then issue the troopers powder and lead."

"We've no choice now but to stay and fight.
They'll cut us to pieces if we take flight.
Besides," he said, "there's nowhere to go.
So we'll stay right here in the Alamo."
With canon and powder for their horns,
Thirty beeves and ninety bushels of corn,
And a spring that in the courtyard flowed,
They felt quite secure in the Alamo.

On February the twenty-third,
Santa Anna by flag of truce sent word:
"Surrender or to the sword be put."
And Travis answered with a canon shot.

From Travis to Smith this note went out:
"The enemy numbers a thousand now.
Send reinforcements, but if you can't,
We'll hold the Alamo to the last man.
I like a soldier shall die," wrote he,
"For honor and Texas and liberty."
These fatal words his temper bespeak:
"I shall never surrender or retreat."

James Butler Bonham, courier brave,
To Goliad rode to enlist their aid;
When he returned to the Alamo,
The message he brought from Fannin was "no."
But in Gonzales, they heard the call
And mustered thirty-two rifles in all.
Under Kimball, to glory they rode,
And fought their way into the Alamo.

As February wore into March,
More and more soldiers arrived at Bexar,
Until three thousand muskets or more
Surrounded a hundred and eighty-four.
Far to the east, on the Brazos bank,
The second of March dawned frigid and damp;
In Washington there, that fateful morn,
The great Republic of Texas was born.

Back in the Alamo on that day,
The sky and the mood of the men were gray.
The enemy, now three thousand strong
And growing, would storm the walls before long.
Then in the blind night a rider sped
With a plea to Fannin at Goliad.
Captain Seguin, bold ambassador,
Succeeded where Bonham had failed before.

James Fannin left the Presidio
With five hundred men for the Alamo;
But four miles out, a wagon broke down,
And Fannin took his army back to town.
(Twenty days later, at Goliad,
James Fannin with four hundred men and staff
Would be massacred - by the same foe
He'd refused to fight at the Alamo.)

G. E. Kruckeberg

The sixth of March dawned misty and cold -
Then Mexican bands struck up "Deguello,"
And Santa Anna's two-hundred score
Advanced on a hundred and eighty four.
For five bloody hours, the battle raged -
Texas rifles against muskets and blades -
And when the gunsmoke had cleared, the score
Was sixteen hundred to one-eighty-four.

Sam Houston avenged the Alamo
On the grassy plains at the San Jacinto;
The future of Texas was secured -
At a cost almost too much to endure.
Bowie, Kimball, Crocket, and Travis,
And those less famous, we promise you this:
As long as there's a Texas, you'll know
We'll honor the men of the Alamo.

FREDERICKSBURG

Ah, to be in Fredericksburg,
Far away from the madding herd,
Amidst the warmth of German cheer
(And German food and German beer),
Where fields and orchards bounty give,
And lovers say, *"Ich liebe dich,"*
And Texas hospitality
Is more than mere formality.

Though it sounds absurd, it's true:
In Fredericksburg the sky's more blue.
(It may just be the clearer air -
Or maybe heaven's closer there.)
The women there are prettier,
And all the men are wittier,
And seldom does an angry word
Disturb the peace in Fredericksburg.

Fredericksburg, where people come
To take a bit of solace from
The wealth of nature's finery
(And Oberhellmann's Winery) -
A place where weary spirits rest,
And Easter fires and *Kinderfest*
Gladden the heart and make old men
Feel just like children once again.

IRVING WALLENSTEIN

Irv Wallenstein was a mother's despair
With his winsome shock of chestnut hair.
He had eyes like coals and teeth like pearls
And one all consuming interest: girls.
While the other boys in grammar school
Were playing ball or playing the fool,
Irv Wallenstein was learning to play
Games that would make him famous some day.
Irv studied girls and learned what to do
To make them do what he wanted them to.
And as he became expert at the game,
His conquests grew, and so did his fame.

In Irving's game of musical maid
His ever popular stock in trade
Was a gift of candies, stale and sweet,
That he bought by the gross in Maxwell Street
Packed in a box he had special made,
Shaped like a heart and flocked in red.
And hardly a maid or matron or wife
To whom he gave a box of that tripe
Who wouldn't have given her hand anon,
But she'd turn her head, and he'd be gone.
(To the fathomless female mind, such cheek
Could naught but add to Irving's mystique.)

Irv's only career in life was women.
He never got rich or preached a sermon
Or wrote a book or did anything
That usually fame or fortune brings.
Yet when, at the age of ninety-four,
He was shot while fleeing a lady's boudoir,
And the word went out that Irving was dead,
A hundred women to nunneries fled.
Fifty or more died by their own hands,
And thousands for months wore black armbands.
And countless others, when they heard he'd died,
Went off to their bedrooms and quietly cried.

38

Then down through the years the legend grew
Of Wallenstein, who to love had been true,
Till hardly a maid, by puberty,
Had not heard the tale at her mother's knee,
Nor gone at night to her bed snug and warm
To dream of sleeping in Wallenstein's arms.
And thousands each year, on the day of his birth,
Would pilgrimage to his small plot of earth,
And there drop a rose, or a tear, or a sigh.
And Irving's birthday, finally,
Was made a national holiday:
February fourteenth, Wallenstein's Day!

G. E. Kruckeberg

THE PARK

In the midst of the city's gray and grime
Is a tawdry patch of faded lime,
Where old men doze in the warm sunshine,
And young lovers stroll with their hands entwined.

There children play in the fresh grass cuttings
'Mid litter left from people's lunchings,
And condoms left from last night's lovings,
And the dried blood stains from last night's muggings.

CREDO

To paraphrase Thoreau (as I've
Been known to on occasion):
The mass of men, it seems, live lives
Of fiat dedication.
The standards of society
They take to be their measure,
And they affect propriety
And trade restraint for pleasure.

From childhood on, we're taught to give
Obedience without question,
And told authority exists
For everyone's protection.
But when the rules are analyzed
We find undue dissension,
And moral strength is compromised
By morals in contention.

We're told how we should think and act
By churches and their minions,
While pundits, with fictitious facts,
Admonish their opinions;
And politicians legislate
Provincial prejudices,
While judges other laws negate
Against the people's wishes.

When regulations contradict,
Can aught be regulated?
And how can strictures aught restrict
When contraindicated?
Can less than chaos be deserved
When mores are conflicting?
And might we not be better served
To do our own restricting?

G. E. Kruckeberg

We all instinctively know right
From wrong and fact from fiction.
Let then your conscience be your guide,
And these be your directions:
"In others see yourself revealed;
Treat them as you'd be treated.
Have patience, and keep pride concealed."
No more than this is needed.

CAUTION

Some people say, "Enjoy your youth.
Get what you can today, because
Tomorrow may not come." They view
Restraint and caution as unjust.
Tomorrow may not come, it's true.
But then again, suppose it does?

Some people say, "Risk and succeed."
But when they fail at any chore,
The say, "The fault was not with me.
Who could have known what was in store?"
It's true the future we can't see,
But isn't that what caution's for?

Some people say, "To get your due,
You've got to be a little blunt.
People will often give to you
What you've the brass to ask up front."
Brass gets you what you ask, that's true,
But caution gets you what you want.

G. E. Kruckeberg

THE LOST WORD

My Daddy always told me, "Live your life
So you won't ever have to apologize."
And though I've one or two times since
Ignored those words, I'm still convinced
The only thing that furthers harmony
In human intercourse is courtesy.

Discourtesy was once a cardinal sin -
A thing that one just didn't do - and then
When liberty and license came,
In people's minds, to mean the same,
We forfeited responsibility,
And with it, any need for courtesy.

The English language has a word for lie,
But none for tell the truth. Do you know why?
A thing that's commonly observed
Has no need of a separate word.
And by the way, these days, it seems to me,
One seldom hears the word "discourtesy."

"Things unused are a burden of great weight;
Each hour can use what it alone creates."
Thus Faust reveals a timeless truth:
A thing will perish through disuse.
And courtesy so seldom is observed
Discourtesy's become a useless word.

HONESTY

"Honesty's the best policy,"
They say, But on reflection,
We can see much animosity
Is prevented by deception.
When our hostess for dinner asks
How we like her new curtains,
We think of truth as a thorny path
Trod only by foolish persons.

Dishonesty's lubricity
Society embraces,
And pretension and duplicity
Are considered social graces.
The truth is a commodity
Much touted - but ill savored,
And it's one of nature's oddities
That by humans it's so favored.

Honesty's not a natural
Condition of our genus,
Nor of any other animal,
Nor even of plants. The Venus
Fly Trap lures with false aroma
It's meal within its clutches;
Chameleons change their very chroma
To resemble rocks or bushes.

Deception is a part of life -
A method of survival.
Can we then honestly be surprised
To observe it in our rivals?
And can we say with honesty
Our word we've never broken,
Or imagine social harmony
Where the truth is always spoken?

G. E. Kruckeberg

Deceit is the oil that prevents
Excessive human friction,
And the truth is: truth's a monkey wrench
In the gears of our convictions.
Expect then not the truth from me,
No more than I from you would;
For it's not the truth shall make you free,
But the kindness of your falsehoods.

REALITY

People make their private hells
Comfortable and propitious;
They decide among themselves,
By what they declare fictitious,
In reality to dwell
Or to live in dreams and wishes.

But our disbelief won't change
Laws of nature or of heaven;
We have got to rearrange
What we've chosen to believe in.
Solving problems is constrained
By ignoring what's been given.

People have a hundred ways
Of denying nature's candor;
Some throw up their hands and say
That no one can understand her.
Some withdraw, and others pray.
Others wild-eyed theories pander.

Some to ancient books appeal,
Some to prophecy and fable.
But this truth will truth reveal
And mysteries make discernible:
The things in this world that are real
Are those that are demonstrable.

This advice to you I give:
If you would be all you could be,
You must in the real world live;
You can be whate'er you would be
If you start out from what is,
Rather than what you think should be.

G. E. Kruckeberg

THE EMPEROR'S CLOTHES

It's popular these days to share
Our disillusionment
By finding imperfection in
Distinguished men and women.
We're most devout at finding fault
In heroines and heroes,
And, true or not, we love to shout:
"The emperor has no clothes."

Some people hero worship see
As something to resist,
And they can see reality
Where it may not exist.
Of piety celebrities
They strip, and common folks
Applaud with glee the pageantry
Of emperors without clothes.

Ben Franklin is accused by this
New cult of disbelievers
Of being aye a British spy,
As well as a deceiver;
And Jefferson, we're told by some,
For all his righteous pose,
Was guilty of a woman's love.
The emperor has no clothes.

George Washington, A paragon
Of virtue and of charm,
Is still suspect, because he kept
Slaves at Mount Vernon farm.
Abe Lincoln's words at Gettysburg,
And even Shakespeare's prose,
Were, some contend, by others penned.
They steal the emperor's clothes.

But icon smashers and hero bashers
Misunderstanding show;
Our idols may have feet of clay,
But we don't want to know.
It's not the weaknesses that speak
To human needs for growth,
But strength to persist when others insist,
"The emperor has no clothes."

For what we need are noble deeds
Our own deeds to inspire,
And rare the man who will not stand
For something he admires.
It takes but greed and jealousy
Our betters to expose,
But it takes justice, faith, and trust
To see the emperor's clothes.

G. E. Kruckeberg

EXPECTATION

Politicians are adept
At promising the moon;
They'll promise you right into debt
If you allow them to.
We'd throw the rascals out, except
We keep hoping they'll come through.
What keeps the people's adulation
Is expectation.

Love's a lot like politics;
Both are games where open
Deceit and honesty are mixed
With hatred and devotion,
And promises will always fix
The promises you've broken.
The secret of a good relation
Is expectation.

Beggars may parade as czars,
True friends may be untrue,
And if you give too quick your heart,
The fault is all with you.
Folks can't be more than what they are,
So just don't expect them to.
The secret of manipulation
Is expectation.

The pleasure's in becoming,
Instead of in became;
Spring's beauty is more stunning
In December than in May,
And the joy of Christmas coming
Is all over Christmas day.
Reality's an imitation
Of expectation.

The secret to great sex appeal
Is knowing what to hide,
And gifts are always wrapped so we'll
Embellish what's inside;
It's not the food that makes the meal
So much as the appetite.
The spice that flavors all sensation
Is expectation.

Each man has a magic wand,
Though most its use neglect.
The things you really focus on
Are things you always get.
We could have everything we want,
But we get what we expect.
The only source of our frustration
Is expectation.

G. E. Kruckeberg

LIFE'S MYSTERY REVEALED

Sages, teachers, poets, and preachers
O'er the centuries have advised
Us poor, sinful, ignorant creatures
On the mysteries of life.

Some say that life is for enjoyment
And the acquisition of things;
Some say that its proper employment
Is to serve a higher being.

Service to others some admonish,
Or to family or to king.
Though each some respite may accomplish,
They all miss the important thing.

For this advice to life will give more
Meaning than all of the above:
"Life is having something to live for,
And having someone to love."

LUCK WILL FOLLOW

We think of luck as quite unplanned,
And we envy those it's found.
But it's not luck that makes the man;
It's the other way around.
Luck doesn't just occur, it's made;
It may sound trite and hollow,
But this advice my Father gave:
Work hard, and luck will follow.

Buying trouble is expensive -
A self-inflicted onus;
For it's well known that worry is
A self-fulfilling promise.
So have no care for health or wealth,
Nor in self-pity wallow.
Expect the best, and to yourself
Be true, and luck will follow.

And never your shortcomings curse,
For though it may alleve you,
Complaining only makes things worse -
And someone might believe you.
You may not be as strong as Zeus
Nor handsome as Apollo,
But you can't win with an excuse.
Have faith, and luck will follow.

Don't worry or complain or fret
About the things you can change,
And neither wish for nor regret
The things you know you can't change.
Just do the best you can, and live
As carefree as a swallow;
The only thing that matters is:
Love life - and luck will follow.

G. E. Kruckeberg

POLEMOS PATER PANTON

Newton's second law tells us each action
Is an equal and opposite reaction.
Thus everything we see, hear, feel, or smell
Exists in opposition to something else,
And reality's a dichotomy
Of opposites reacting mutually:
You can't have a God without a Satan,
And you can't have a Hell without salvation.

The second law of thermodynamics
Tells us decay is a fact of mechanics:
Reality's more than interaction -
The whole damn universe is in retraction!
But if there's a force that decrees decay,
Then there must be an opposite force at play,
For forces never exist by themselves -
They're always a reaction to something else.

Creativity is that something else,
And its sole embodiment is life itself,
For life is always new growth creating;
It's self-evolving and self-replicating.
All possibilities lie inside us,
If we hark to the words of Heraclitus:
"Nothing is ever achieved without strife."
And that, I suggest, is the secret of life.

REASON

Reason is a goddess
With empty temples, for
Though men may sing her praises,
They worship folly more.
(Even her priests and priestesses
Her altars oft ignore.)

Youth has but one vision:
A lusty passion play.
In love's neurotic prison,
Reason is locked away,
And genital decisions
Are the order of the day.

Anger is a passion
More dangerous than lust.
Yet oft to its attraction
We yield because we must,
For reason is irrational
When justice is unjust.

Danger triggers panic
That quenches reason's light
And leads into the frantic
Activity of fright.
And as we flee from sanity,
Reason is put to flight.

Reason's a delusion -
A mental trick that we
Use to support conclusions
We've reached instinctively,
And to create illusions
Of superiority.

55

G. E. Kruckeberg

LOGIC

The Greeks invented logic,
An aristocratic game -
A pastime philosophic
With a convoluted name.
"The studying of study"
Is what logic means in Greek;
It's as circular a subject
As you'd ever hope to meet.

It leads to false conclusions
Based on premises of air;
It fosters our confusion
And propensity to err.
Life, though, is empirical;
If disaster we'd avert,
The question's not "What's logical?"
The question's "What will work?"

Logic is a closed system
Using only what is known;
It always begs the question
And it always stands alone.
But what of human progress
Has been logically achieved?
We advance by errors, aimless
And illogically perceived.

Christiaan Huygens in chapel
Censer-pendulums discerned,
And Isaac Newton's apple
Taught us how the planets turn,
Could Goodyear's sulphur-rubber
Have been logically deduced?
And could Fleming's famous culture
Have been logically produced?

A logical decision
Is a freedom-robbing thief,
For logic is a prison
Built of obsolete beliefs.
And success does not consist
Of defending our contentions,
But of going beyond logic
To discovery and invention.

G. E. Kruckeberg

THE LAWS OF PERVERSITY

The first law of perversity
Inspires at least a curse a day:
"No matter where a thing's been put,
It's always in the last place you look."

The second law is more perverse,
And it can make a preacher curse:
"If you throw anything away,
You'll need it on the very next day."

The third law of perversity
Discloses nature's perfidy:
"If you've two choices, you will find
You'll choose the wrong one every dang time."

The fourth law of perversity:
"If you drive in to work each day,
The only time you'll get there late
Is when you've called a meeting for eight."

The fifth law of perversity
Is cause for much adversity:
"The less one knows about a thing,
The more he thinks he know everything."

The sixth law of perversity
Works also in vice-versity:
"The things that you're prepared to face
Are the things that never do take place
(And all the things you least expect
Are the ones that happen, sure as heck.)"

SOME PEOPLE

Some people live inside their heads.
They listen to the plots and lies
Of their own thoughts. It might be said
They're more concerned with living than with life.
Some people in the future live,
And some with life the past endow.
But past and future don't exist!
The only time you'll ever have is now.

Some people live by rule and rote,
But life goes on outside a man.
The world is a kaleidoscope,
And you must seize each image while you can.
Those trees have never looked the same
As in this light; we view each day
New clouds that never will again
Those same capricious shapes and hues display.

Each sight and smell and sound's unique.
You hold each moment only once,
And each experience is complete.
Analysis the soul's perception blunts.
So take the joys and leave the rest;
You're soon enough bereft of them.
You've thirty thousand days at best,
And this is the first of the last of them.

G. E. Kruckeberg

DREAMS

Dreams -
Some think of men as schemers.
Others see us as redeemers.
But the truth is we're just dreamers,
For the grass is always greener
In our dreams.

Dreams -
Their lure of evanescent
visions is a human penchant,
And aristocrat and peasant
Both reshape the mundane present
With their dreams.

Dreams -
By God they were intended
Our divinity to hint at,
For our vision is extended
And the future is invented
In our dreams.

Dreams -
By vanity infested -
By reality untested -
From ennui our souls they've wrested,
And our sanity is vested
In our dreams.

Dreams -
Our persuasions they befit,
For life's as our dreams conceive it,
And each deed's as they decree it,
And the world is as we see it
In our dreams.

THAT'S REALITY

People say what a man can't feel
Or see must not be real;
And most of what a man believes,
They say, is fantasy.
But man reality creates
With courage, not with faith.
Just decide how it ought to be -
And that's reality.

People say man is made of mud,
Or, some say, flesh and blood;
Others say that divinity
Is man's consistency.
You can be either lowly mud
Or else a lower god;
Just decide what you want to be -
And that's reality.

People say you're a lovely sort -
A winner and good sport;
Others accuse you of deceit,
Of hatred or conceit.
You can fit any mold, my friend,
With no need to pretend:
Just decide who you want to be -
And that's reality.

You can be miserable as sin
And blame the place you're in,
Or you can be joyful and free -
And in the same place be.
Happiness is a place, it's true;
The place, though, is in you.
Just decide where you want to be -
And that's reality.

G. E. Kruckeberg

VIEWPOINTS

The world is made of many
different people and beliefs:
From spendthrifts to pinchpennies -
From holy men to thieves.
And everyone's incentive
Is gaining inner peace.
We each believe in any
Thing we happen to believe.

The critic has a vision
Of perfecting everyone;
The pragmatist's position
Is take life as it comes.
Thus each of their decisions
And judgments is foregone.
The things that we believe in
Are the things that we become.

The major goal of living
Is confirming self-deceit;
Our views are self-fulfilling
Because they're preconceived.
And each man is perceived in
The things that he perceives.
Seeing is believing,
But we see what we believe.

PERSPECTIVES

When I was ten years old,
The world was made of bold
And fearless games
And dreams of fame
And never growing old.
Good friends were brave and true,
And everybody knew
The most important
Thing was sports;
The second: being cool.

When I was seventeen,
My life was made of dreams
Of lithesome waifs
In lace shirtwaists
And pony tails and jeans.
We found the world unjust,
And love was mixed with lust,
And everything
That life would bring
Was still ahead of us.

When I was twenty-two,
I was convinced I knew
All that there is
To know of this
Old world, and I was through
With colleges and schools
(The young are such damn fools),
And life was all
Mechanical,
If one obeyed the rules.

G. E. Kruckeberg

When I was thirty-six,
My life was filled with kids
And kites and bikes
And scout troop hikes
And things for me to fix.
The world was small in size:
Kids, job, friends, house, and wife.
Then one by one
The kids were gone,
And I was forty-five.

When I was fifty-two,
The world was borne anew -
A world made just
For two of us,
And shared with but a few.
Our life was free and clear,
And fun was our career.
We bought a new
Sports car and flew
To Mexico each year.

Now I am sixty-five
And still in love with life.
For life is growth,
And I am loath
At old age to arrive.
The world still throbs with new
Exciting things to do,
And one can live
Their whole life if
They've something to live through.

FOUR SEASONS

In the enchanted Spring of life,
We focus on impressing
The opposite sex. We think of life
In terms of our possessing
The pleasurable things of life,
And never count our blessings.

Then in life's robust Summer time,
Our days are spent in working,
And responsibilities, we find,
Leave us no time for shirking,
And in the corners of the mind
Is desperation lurking.

In the gay Autumn of our lives,
Repose for pride we barter,
And a calm contentment now arrives
To cool our youthful ardor,
And we observe, to our surprise,
That everything gets harder.

Then in life's pale, gray Winter phase,
The flush of Autumn slumbers,
And memories of more urgent days
Are all that's left of summer.
Yet, when your head your heart obeys,
You swear you're getting younger.

G. E. Kruckeberg

CHOICES

The springtime of our youth
Is a time for making choices;
And we each to different voices
Hark and different courses choose.
Some to social status climb,
Some raise families, some make fortunes,
Some have babies (or abortions),
Some embrace a life of crime.

It's not heredity
Or environment that makes us
What we are, nor stars that take us
To our final destiny.
It's not karma, luck, or fate
That's brought us to this condition,
But the natural attrition
Of the choices that we make.

Each action that we take
To our character a brick adds,
For the soul is very quick at
Justifying its mistakes.
"If I did it, it was right,"
Is the credo of the ego,
And the things today that we do
Chart our actions throughout life.

The choices that we make
Are the choices we must live with,
For the future freedom giveth
But the past doth freedom take.
And life is but a process
Of eliminating options,
And the path of our adoption
We must follow unto death.

UNTIL THE GAME IS OVER

However swiftly you may run,
Outdistancing all others,
However far you may have come
And to your goal come closer,
Though you're ahead, you haven't won
Until the game is over.

And if you count yourself among
The shakers and the movers -
If you're obsessed with number one
And can't abide a loser -
Remember that you haven't won
Until the game is over.

If opportunity or lust
Should tempt a constant lover,
Don't count the effort or the cost
Her virtue to recover.
And don't give up; you haven't lost
Until the game is over.

When trouble like an albatross
Around you seems to hover,
Just grit your teeth and bear the cross
You're given like a soldier,
And ne'er forget: you haven't lost
Until the game is over.

For fate may triumph or despair
Bestow without disclosure;
And whether life be foul or fair,
You must keep your composure.
Just smile a lot and hang in there
Until the game is over.

G. E. Kruckeberg

FIRST TIMES

I'll never forget
The first girl who let
Me kiss her, when I was just nine.
'Though I've kissed others since, I remember best
The magic of that first time.

And I can recall
As if it had all
Happened only a week ago
My first deer, the first time I drank alcohol,
And the first cigar I smoked.

We all reminisce
About our first kiss -
The first time we fought or made love,
But some of our best first times don't yet exist:
The ones we're still dreaming of.

So don't be dismayed,
And don't be afraid
Of things unfamiliar or strange.
In loving or fighting or plying your trade,
The name of the game is change.

And if you should see
Opportunity,
And you want to give it a fling,
Don't worry, just do it, 'cause there's got to be
A first time for everything.

SECOND CHANCES

In games of chance or games of skill,
You've never lost until you quit.
You get to try your luck until
You win, or lose, or tire of it.
But in life's harsher circumstances,
You don't get second chances.

The game of life is never won;
Each day begins a brand new game.
If you don't move ahead, my son,
You're sure to fall behind again,
And watch as someone else advances.
Don't wait for second chances.

The game of love is played for keeps,
And if you play and fail to win,
You're left with mem'ries incomplete
And ghosts of things that might have been.
For broken dreams and dead romances,
There are no second chances.

So when you play the game, don't fret
About the chances lost or marred.
Remember that, to get ahead,
You've got to start from where you are.
Don't waste your time with backward glances.
You don't get second chances.

And when the game of life is o'er,
And you look back on what you've done,
You'll surely wish that you'd done more -
Had spread more joy - had had more fun,
And done more things that life enhances.
We don't get second chances.

G. E. Kruckeberg

So do whate'er you want to do,
And do it now, while you still can.
For when the reaper beckons you,
You know there'll be no second chance.
To this refrain the whole world dances:
There are no second chances.

KEEP TRYING

When it seems you just can't win,
And you get tired of vying
With people who just won't give in,
Keep trying.

When you're sick and tired of life,
And you're convinced that dying
Would be a blessing in disguise,
Keep trying.

Don't ever get discouraged
When life won't do your biding.
Losing always takes more courage
Than quitting.

When you think you can't go on,
And you just feel like crying,
It's just the dark before the dawn.
Keep trying.

Let this be your attitude:
"Keep trying till you get it."
'Cause if you don't swing at it, you
Can't hit it.

So, my friend, keep swinging true,
For there is no denying
Your dreams will all come true if you
Keep Trying.

G. E. Kruckeberg

PLAY THE GAME

When I was lad playing football
At Warren G. Harding High School,
My coach was old Jonathan Goodall,
And Coach Goodall had just one rule.
His constant locker room refrain
Was, "Play the game, boys, play the game."

In business, when I wonder, "could all
These people be other than fools?"
I think of Coach Jonathan Goodall
And remember his golden rule.
And that rule keeps me safe and sane:
Just play the game, boy, play the game.

In love, or its surrogate, passion,
A man's got to learn to give in.
Don't argue about her infractions;
You'll lose, whether you lose or win.
It's not important who's to blame.
Just play the game, boy, play the game.

In life, with its infinite problems,
If you'll concentrate on each play,
You'll find that, like Halloween goblins,
Your worries will vanish away.
It's not your purpose to complain.
Just play the game, boy, play the game.

And though it be late in fourth quarter,
Keep playing till you hear the gun.
The game's never lost till it's over;
The game's never won till it's done.
You're still becoming, not became,
So play the game, boy, play the game.

To take credit would be dishonest
For all life has given to me.
Success was assured in the promise
Of Coach Goodall's great legacy,
And to my sons I leave the same:
Just play the game, boys, play the game.

G. E. Kruckeberg

GOOD ADVICE

Good advice is hard to find;
You mostly get the other kind.
But my advice so much excels
I sometimes even take it myself!
So let me give you, free and clear,
The benefit of sixty odd years.

Married life can be sublime,
If you'll just keep one thing in mind:
Whatever sort of game she's in,
A woman has always got to win.
So don't ever argue with your wife
(Unless you like the monastic life).

Trouble seldom sets a snare,
But if you look for it, it's there.
A man has got to understand
The first precept of being a man:
Don't run from trouble, whatever you do,
But stand upwind of a man that chews.

Before you hurt somebody else,
Make sure it's not to please yourself.
Don't do it just because it's fun,
Don't do it just to impress someone,
Don't do it just to prove you're a man,
And don't do it just because you can.

If you want to keep your friends,
Don't ever give advice to them.
If your advice ill luck should spawn,
They'll surely blame you for being wrong;
And if they profit from your advice,
They'll blame you then because you were right.

BE TRUE TO YOURSELF

Don't brag and boast or count the cost
Of what you've done for others.
As you mature, you may be sure
That one day you'll discover
You don't do things for someone else;
You do them for yourself.

Good friends are scarce and true love's rare.
Both must be cultivated.
Gripe not nor scold, or you'll grow old
Alone - but vindicated!
When you attack somebody else,
You hurt only yourself.

Blame others not for what you've wrought,
Nor let your pride deceive you.
A man must make his own mistakes.
Besides, no one believes you.
To implicate somebody else
Is but to fool yourself.

I've never known a dog so dumb
He couldn't say, "I love you."
Some people, with great verbal gifts,
Can only blame and cuss you.
But you can't love somebody else
If you don't like yourself.

Let not your words take flight to hurt
Nor self-restraint forsake you;
Rudeness a slight cannot make right -
But it can slighter make you.
When you embarrass someone else,
You shame only yourself.

G. E. Kruckeberg

STABILITY

Though stability's the stated ambition
Of every pundit and politician,
The ones who know how to achieve it are rare.
But as every good engineer is aware,
Stability is just a condition
Of stresses balanced in opposition.

A coalition is a concoction
Of forces bent on their own destruction,
And consensus is premised on compromise
(Its very conception assures its demise);
In politics, as in all life's functions,
Stability is never an option.

Most people accept life's diversity
And flow with the currents of history,
But no current ever can eddies avert;
Some people see progress as just too much work.
It seems that what we call stability
Is often the fear of activity.

HUMAN NATURE

People are so evident!
It's easy to see what they want.
Whether it's money, spouse, or job,
They always want just what you've got.
And they are such a friendly lot
(As long as they want what you've got),
But give them money, power, or fame,
And suddenly they forget your name.

People always act straight-laced,
But actually they're all two-faced;
The things that they blame others for
They do themselves behind closed doors.
And they all have this telling trait:
They always will congratulate
You after you succeed, but they'll
Never forewarn you before you fail.

People have such damnable
Conceit they're self-programmable;
They don't judge you by what you do
But by what they expect you to.
They cast the world in images
Projected by their prejudice,
And everything they hear and see
Is only what they want it to be.

People are so gullible!
They fill their heads with fanciful
Religions, legends, dreams of sex,
And fairy tales and politics.
For they'll believe most anything
That promises relief to bring
From the great curse of humankind:
The boredom of an uncluttered mind.

G. E. Kruckeberg

THE HAND

The hand is a wonderful instrument;
Its versatility
Defines the crowning complement
Of our humanity.
A hand can make an apple pie
Or set a broken bone.
A hand can make a lover sigh,
And a hand can fire a gun.

A hand can write beautiful symphonies
That multitudes enthrall,
Or it can write obscenities
On subway station walls.
The human hand can make a fist
Or mold an earthen jar,
And anthropologists insist
It's made us what we are.

"Behold the wondrous opposable thumb,"
They tell us. "It's unique."
(Gorillas, though, have four of them,
And two are on their feet!)
Now, could it be misguided
Anthropology assigned
The credit to the human hand
Instead of the human mind?

The hand is a marvelous instrument,
But instrument it is.
It's just a tool to implement
Directions that we give.
It has no morals and no will,
So neither blame nor praise
Whate'er it does for good or ill,
For the hand is but a slave.

ACTORS AND CRITICS

All the world's a stage, they say,
And life is all theatrics,
But some are actors in the play,
And others only critics.
The actors are the ones who get
Things done and make things better,
While critics only denigrate
The actors and director.

Actors never do complain;
They play the parts assigned them
And modestly accept acclaim.
Their faults they put behind them.
But critics try to justify
Their failures by detracting
From others, for to criticize
Is easier than acting.

Critics almost never praise
The plays that pass before them;
If they find nothing bad to say,
They'll often just ignore them.
But actors complement the play
With lines of guileless cunning,
And if there's nothing good to say,
They'll simply make up something.

Actors can make even bad
scripts come alive with splendor.
(They make things happen, I might add,
With acting, not with candor.)
But critics view with jaundiced eyes
The whole theatric milieu,
And sedulously criticize
The things they think they can't do.

G. E. Kruckeberg

So be an actor, not a snit.
Success is all in your hands.
Just act your part, follow the script,
And play to your audience.
Forget the plot; the play's the thing.
Enjoy the part you're given.
The next act brings what it must bring;
The script's already written.

WINNERS AND LOSERS

Losers think that they're the best,
But that, by others, they're oppressed.
They rend their clothes and tear their hair
And make excuses everywhere.
From losers 'round the world is heard:
"Life is a four-letter word."

Winners think that they're the best,
And they set out to prove it, lest
They waste, in self-defeating strife,
One moment of this gift of life.
For winners know, beyond a doubt,
That life is what it's all about.

G. E. Kruckeberg

BITCHERS

Some folks sit on their posteriors
And make themselves out to be superior
By pointing out self-righteously
Mistakes that're made by their enemies.
(And enemies they never lack;
Their attitude assures them of that.)
This is their credo, never flouted:
"Don't fix it if you can bitch about it."

But those who moan and bitch and frown
And build themselves up by pulling us down
Do more than hurt the common good;
They show by their bitching that they're dead wood.
For those who work and take the risks
Have neither the need nor time to bitch.
They're too busy making our lives richer.
So let's be fixers instead of bitchers.

CONTENTMENT

In this old world of sadness,
There's nothing sadder than
A man who labors daily
At a job he cannot stand.
His tragic life is shortened
By bitterness and hate,
And those around him suffer as
He long laments his fate.

But in this world of conflict,
There's no one more content
Than the man who loves his job,
For he follows his own bent.
And people pay him money
For doing what he likes;
He's never had to work a day
In his entire life.

If you like what you're doing,
Then you'll like who you are;
There'll be a spring in your step
And a lightness in your heart.
For life consists of action,
And action molds our views;
And you're not what you say you are,
You're only what you do.

G. E. Kruckeberg

SOCIALISM

Some people say,
"If the world were like me,
Oh, what a wonderful
World it would be!
There'd be no dissension
Or enmity,
For we'd all be so much
Alike, you see."

But if we were all
Like peas in a pod -
From the same pattern
And of the same cloth -
I think the world would be
Frighteningly odd,
With no need for love
And no place for God.

PARASITES

Everyone's got
To work for a livin'
But prostitutes, preachers,
And politicians.

Prostitutes truly
Enjoy what they sell,
And preachers enjoy
Damning people to hell.

And all politicians
Love selling themselves.
Not one of the three
Would do anything else.

But this is the thing
That's really disgusting:
We pay them for doing
What they'd do for nothing.

G. E. Kruckeberg

ENGINEERS

Engineers are rather weird;
They think in cranks and gears and such.
They ply their trade with smoke and mirrors.
(Or so it seems to most of us.)

Engineers can be a bore
(Although they're honest to a fault);
They'll tell you all they know and more!
(Or maybe they just like to talk.)

Engineers need challenges;
If problems they don't have enough,
They'll keep their mental balances
By simply making problems up.

Engineers are quite content;
They never get upset, it seems,
And stress, to them's, what makes the bend
They calculate in columns and beams.

Engineers are curious blokes;
They're always taking things apart
And reading articles and books
(Instead of practicing their art).

Engineers can be inventive;
In fact, their genius runs amok
When their principal incentive
Is fixing something they screwed up.

ACCOUNTANTS

Accountants are a stodgy lot.
Although they've traded their ink pots
And ledgers for today's computers,
They haven't gotten any astuter.

They still insist, as they did when
Accountants used a goose quill pen,
On twice recording every dime.
(It seems such a terrible waste of time!)

Accountants worship their traditions
And have no patience with omissions.
The most important thing of all
Is to follow accounting ritual.

Creativity is not a
Thing accountants have a lot of.
(They can't afford it, truth to tell;
Creative accountants end up in jail.)

Accountants like to measure things,
But unlike engineers, they think
Of measurement less as a goal
Than a means of giving them more control.

Accountability's a word
Accountants use a lot, I've heard.
It means: if something should go wrong,
You've got to have someone to blame it on.

G. E. Kruckeberg

MAINTENANCE

Maintenance is a private clan;
No one but a maintenance man
Knows all the secrets and the tricks
That are required machines to fix.

But one could learn, if one were made
Privy to the maintenance trade,
How to fix things that are broke
(Or even how to cuss and smoke).

If you should like to learn to fix
Things, you could surely benefit
From a spell in Maintenance.
Here's one you may have heard, perchance:

"Hocus Pocus! Alakazam!
Thunder and lightning! Hell and damn!
You stupid, worthless pile of tin,
Fix yourself or I'll kick you again!"

MANAGEMENT

Managers are people who
Give other people work to do.
They delegate most everything
(Except, perhaps, their breathing).
They don't have time for work, it's true:
They're always in a meeting.

Management is such a chore -
You never quite know what you're for
Or what you ought to be against
(Except, of course, the offense).
And straddling the fence won't work,
'Cause they keep moving the fence.

Managers invariably
Operate procedurally.
This their motto is: "Do nothing
If it's not approved in ink;
Don't do anything that's risky
Or that makes you have to think."

Managers can manage stuff
That they know very little of.
They consequently get things done
By giving people freedom.
(If managers don't add that much,
Why do we really need 'em?)

Managers are paid to be
Responsible and trustworthy.
(Accountable's another name
Often used to mean the same.)
And *that's* why managers we need:
Someone's got to take the blame.

G. E. Kruckeberg

THE FISHERMEN

A business is like a fishing trip,
And each member of the crew
Is responsible for the success of it
Through the job they have to do.

Engineering's job is cutting bait,
And Production runs the ship;
Management sets a course that's safe
And Accounting cleans the fish.

But the most important department -
The reason the others exist -
Is Sales, for they are the fishermen;
Without them, we'd have no fish.

SEVEN DAYS

Sunday is a day of ease;
It eases us into the week.
We mow the yard
And wash the car,
And suddenly it's Monday eve.
Some say that life's
Too short, but I've
Found life is long enough, at least;
It's just the weekends are too brief.

Monday is a day of rest;
We stand around the coffee mess
For half the day
And hear replays
Of all of Sunday's sports contests.
We leave at five
And wonder why
On Mondays we accomplish less.
(It must just be the weather, we guess.)

Tuesday is a day of toil;
From Monday's doldrums we recoil.
We slave all day
Without a break,
And then take more work home to moil.
For what was Monday
Left undone
We now burn Tuesday's midnight oil
(And Tuesday's television spoil).

Wednesday is a day of hope,
With both weekends within our scope.
We can't slow down,
But still somehow
Midweek it's easier to cope
With folks who fuss
And harry us
To keep pushing the envelope.
(At least we're on the downhill slope.)

Thursday is the day of truth;
You've got a million things to do
Before this week
Is history,
And everybody's after you
With something else;
You tell yourself
You're never going to make it through.
And then, somehow, you finally do.

Friday is a day of joy,
And nothing can our mood destroy,
For Saturday
Is on the way,
And just the thought our spirits buoy.
It's too late to
Start something new,
For should our efforts we deploy,
We'd expectation less enjoy.

Saturday's a day of play,
And Monday seems a month away.
But whether loafing,
Playing golf,
Or barbecuing beef fillets,
Old *deja vu*
Is haunting you,
For you know that in just two days
You'll have to run the same rat race.

ECONOMIC ANIMALS

Mars was not of religion born,
Nor was the sword of Arthur
Forged to protect all Christendom,
Or curb misguided ardor.
Religion and stupidity
Are naught but war's excuses;
It's only our cupidity
The course of conflict chooses.

The Holy Land crusades were fought
For trade routes and for spices;
The War Between the States was caused
By falling cotton prices.
Wars are always fought for freedom
And liberty, it's a fact:
The freedom people to steal from,
And the liberty to tax.

Nor does the course of commerce prove
To be more philanthropic;
There's nothing that it wouldn't use
To maximize its profits.
And those of altruistic bent
Are even less attendant:
Religion, law, and medicine
Are all profit-dependent.

From government to industry -
From geniuses to dummies -
The goal of all humanity
Is simply making money,
And whether frivolous or grave -
Whether tragic or comic -
All of our decisions are made
For reasons economic.

93

G. E. Kruckeberg

VERBOSITY

To this advice I hew
With importunate tenacity:
Sedulously eschew
Polysyllabic loquacity.

WHEN YOU WERE MINE

Fog is deep beneath the pines,
And the pale moon softly shines
On the temple gate atop the hill.
All the world is silent and my heart is still
As I think back to a time when you were mine.

Winds of change and sands of time
Turn the rivers of the mind.
Yet their empty beds remain to show
Where the quiet, moonlit waters used to flow
In another life and time when you were mine.

I must live though I am blind
To the pleasures of mankind,
And when life is gone, I know there'll be
Memories to haunt me through eternity,
And I'll know there was a time when you were mine.
There will always be a time when you were mine.

WHEN I SAW HER FACE

When I saw her face for the first time,
Spring was in the air.
The sun was weaving gold in her hair.
She was more alive than the birds
And younger than the flowers.
We used to talk for hours
Until the dawn would creep
Like a thief through her window.
She meant more to me than she meant to,
And I loved much more than I cared.
Then when the summer was over,
She left me with memories of all of the good times
And all of the dreams we had dared -
And the love that we shared.

When I saw her face for the last time,
Leaves were brown and gold.
Her trembling lips were red from the cold.
As she turned to go, I could see
A teardrop in her eye.
Then for a moment I
Held her in my embrace
With her face in my shoulder.
I knew I would never again
Hold her as I held her that day.
I knew that summer was over,
But still I regret all the things that I wanted
To tell her but just didn't say,
As I watched her walk away.

G. E. Kruckeberg

THE OPPOSITE SEX

Women, we say, are the opposite sex –
A term that elicits confusion.
What we mean by opposite, I suspect,
Is opposite from our delusions.

Women, we say, are egotistical,
But the fault is not wholly with them.
It's true that women think about themselves,
But they get a lot of help from men.

Women, we say, are exhibitionists
And pander to masculine voyeurs.
But if men weren't so damn voyeuristic,
Women would be more modest, I'm sure.

Women, we say, are thoughtless and shallow,
But what chance would men have to survive
All the troubles and strife of life's battles
Without mothers and sisters and wives?

Women, we say, are from Adam's rib wrought,
But my own observations suggest
That women were made in the image of God,
And that men are the opposite sex.

96

I LIKE WOMEN

I like women.
I admire their grace and style.
And it never fails to intrigue
Me when they say, "Now aren't you sweet?"
And it makes my heart skip a beat when they smile.
I like women - but I'm not beguiled.

I like women.
I like lighting their cigarettes.
And I like the way they excite me
And how their glances invite me
To do what I know I'd likely regret.
I like women - but not to excess.

I like women.
I like helping them with their coats.
And I like the way that they smell
And the way they pout when they're jealous
And how they blush when they're telling a joke.
I like women – But not up too close.

I like women.
I like buying them beer and wine.
And I like the way that they laugh
And the way they look from the back,
And I like the things that they have on their minds.
I like women - but I'm not inclined.

I like women.
I like gazing into her eyes.
And I like the way she gets miffed
When she needs a hug and a kiss
And the way her eyes always shift when she lies.
I like women – and I love my wife.

G. E. Kruckeberg

WOMEN

Women are a
Breed apart. The
Things they do are most amusing.
They get mad,
Though, if you laugh.
Women are confusing.

Women always
Get their own ways,
And you better never cross 'em!
If you try,
They start to cry!
Women are a caution!

Women bitch to
us, but if you
Grouse when they do something frightful,
They just say,
"Don't be that way."
Women are delightful!

Women never
Were too clever
At the things that men are good at,
So they just
Rely on us.
Women are not stupid.

When you're busy
Watching TV,
They'll waltz by in something sexy.
When you're ready,
They get a headache!
Women drive me crazy!

In their teeny
Tight bikinis,
With bare thighs and legs and tummies,
They walk by us
Looking pious.
Women are so funny!

Women like to
Flirt, but if you
Get caught getting what they promised,
They'll complain
That you're to blame.
Women are dishonest!

But when all is
Said and done it's
Women that make life worth living.
That's 'cause what
We need they've got,
And they're all for giving.

G. E. Kruckeberg

LIFE IS NOW

Belabor not your conscience with self-censure;
Regret will oft beget its own regret.
Nor yearn for people or for things that once were,
For life is now, and yesterday is dead.

Dwell not on what may happen on the morrow,
Nor waste your time with plots and plans and schemes.
And borrow neither future joy nor sorrow,
For life is now; tomorrow's but a dream.

So sing no dirges for lost love or labor,
Nor anthems raise to things that may yet be,
But celebrate the one thing we can savor:
This single instant of eternity.

THE TEN COMMANDMENTS

Some say Church and State should be one.
"Our laws," they say, "are based upon
The Ten Commandments given by
God to Moses on Mount Sinai."
But those who foster this delusion
Do more than flout the Constitution;
By this inaccurate recital,
They show they've never read the bible.
For this important fact they've missed:
The Ten Commandments don't exist!
In Exodus twenty, we find
That God gave Moses only nine.

G. E. Kruckeberg

GOD

Functionally, religions are
Secular institutions.
Their object is conformity;
Their bane is evolution.
Souls are saved by obedience
And damned by innovation,
And only priests can speak for God
And broker your salvation.
And everything that can be known
Of God and everything else
Is in some ancient sacred text
That was written by God himself.

But God is not in the Bible,
Nor is He in the Koran.
God is in every act and thought
Of every woman and man.
The fool has said, "There is no god!"
The wise man says, "This is true:
There is no god outside yourself,
For God lives only through you."
God is our common consciousness;
God is life and strife and love.
To paraphrase Pogo Possum:
"We have found God and He is us."

GET OUT OF YOUR HEAD

Powerful is the intellect;
It well deserves our praise.
But grant it not your worship lest
It make of you its slave.
"The tool is not the master," 'tis said.
Get out of your head.

The incessant cacophony
Of human thinking drives
With self-fulfilling sophistry
The essence from our lives
'Til not thinking is a thing we dread.
Get out of your head.

For what we think's not what we are.
The human spirit soars
Above the mind and reaches far
Beyond its mundane chores.
And on quiet is that spirit fed.
Get out of your head.

The mind is focused on itself -
Its future and its past;
The soul's content to simply dwell
Right when and where it's at.
To never be anxious or afraid,
Get out of your head.

The part of man that really lives
Is not between his ears.
The mind will die; the spirit is
Untouched by death or years.
To live forever after you're dead,
Get out of your head.

G. E. Kruckeberg

KARMA

Some say to kill a murderer
Is unusual and cruel.
(But if he killed somebody first,
It can't be unusual!)
And it's not as cruel to kill him
For a crime that's capital
As for him to kill his victim
For no damn reason at all.
Besides, by all the rules of fate,
You must die the way you lived.
You have to give back what you take
And you get back what you give.

Some people live their life as if
They're the only one on earth.
In business, love, and politics,
Number one always comes first.
Rules to them are a travesty –
They make their own, they believe.
Then through divorce and tragedy,
They loudly complain, "Why me?"
The rules of life you can't negate,
And the first rule of life is:
You've got to give back what you take
And you get back what you give.

We all know people who will n'er
Achieve great fame or fortune
They always do more than their share
And take the smaller portion.
But their fame is in their giving,
And their wealth is in their friends,
And they know that life's worth living
And that death is not the end.
The Law of Karma we can state
Another way, and that is:
Always give back more than you take
And you'll get back what you give.

SEX

Some say women are from Venus,
And from Mars descends the rest.
Men are reduced to a penis -
Women to the bridge between us
And our fantasies of sex.

Gender differences divide us;
That's a truth I won't contest.
But the standard that unites us
And the magic that excites us
Is our common need for sex.

Sex is an undercurrent of
All human interaction -
Of competition, hate, and love.
And social mechanisms move
By physical attraction.

We've invented gods to dote on,
And our psyche is complex.
But the source of all devotion
And the reason for emotion
Is our love affair with sex.

Some find food a substitution
For frustrated dreams of sex.
But eons of evolution
Echo this forgone conclusion:
Food is good, but sex is best.

Some seek wealth and some seek station;
Some for fame or beauty quest.
But looking past these machinations,
We see the basic motivation
Of the human race is sex.

G. E. Kruckeberg

YOU DON'T HAVE TO GET OLD

As we our burdens shoulder
Down the last mile of road
Toward where our bones will moulder
In the earth's eternal fold,
We must face life like soldiers –
Courageous, young, and bold –
And never let the odor
Of idleness taint our souls,
Nor let resentment smoulder,
Nor fear our passions mold,
But cultivate exposure
To new ideas and modes.
For youth is the beholder
Of things beyond its bode,
And age but well-worn boulders
Of habit that youth erodes.
Then, like George Burns, discover
The wisdom he extolled:
"You can't help getting older,
But you don't have to get old."

THE CHEMICAL SOLUTION

For every malady and pain
There's a specific medicine.
For impotence and allergies
And vitamin deficiencies
And eyes that're burned red by pollution
We have a chemical solution.

It started in the twenties when
Bayer invented aspirin,
And through the years we steadily
Progressed from herbal remedies
And keeping a healthy constitution
To the chemical solution.

We no longer worry about
The things that we put in out mouths,
Or whether we exercise or not.
We let our bodies go to pot.
For our sins we have an absolution.
We have a chemical solution

One out of five commercials on
TV these days is pushing some
Pill or potion for something that
We never even knew we had.
It's an economic revolution
Of pharmaceutical solutions.

As soon as we feel slightly ill,
We drink some glop or pop some pill.
We never let the body do
The things that it was programmed to,
And a billion years of evolution
Is swamped in chemical solutions.

Pyridoxine, vitamin C,
And other chemicals we need
For life we used to make ourselves.
Now we must get them someplace else.
Because of their past massive infusions,
We have lost the need to produce them.

The body changes constantly,
Adapting to the chemistry
Of the milieu on which it feeds,
Producing only what it needs.
Thus do our potions and prescriptions
Define our future malnutrition.

WIZARD WITHOUT A WAND

He was born in nineteen-twenty-six
And never cared much for politics.
But then, in nineteen-seventy-four,
He was advisor to President Ford.
He advised Presidents Reagan, Clinton,
George the First, and George the Second.
And though his advice was good (he claimed),
It never did make much of a change.

For more than sixteen years, he served
As Chairman of the Federal Reserve.
His puppet was the interest rate
(The one thing he could manipulate).
And though he moved it all around,
From side to side and up and down,
It never had much effect, it seems,
On the U. S. economy.

But Economics is proficient
At explanation, not prediction;
It has been called the science of
Belaboring past occurrences.
Ronald Reagan's description was true:
An Economist is someone who
Sees a thing work in practice and worries
Whether or not it'll work in theory.

It's said that Economics is
The whore of modern politics.
And this artifice defines them both:
"Just saying a thing will make it so."
Economists posture and pretend
That their decisions have great portent.
But Economics, it seems to me,
Is the creature of the economy.

G. E. Kruckeberg

LIBERALS

Though *Fountainhead* aspired
To strangle with satire
Egalitarianism,
Ellsworth Toohey is still,
It seems, alive and well
And living in Washington.

Collectivists are all
Now known as Liberals,
And no one calls them Commies,
Still, in the final cut,
A Liberal is just
A Socialist with money.

All Liberals are averse
To bell-shaped Gausian curves
And logical conclusions;
They spend their time on schemes
For redistributing
The normal distribution.

But to ignore the course
Of history is worse
Than not to know it's changing,
And this sin greater yawns:
To spend our taxes on
History rearranging.

For lost causes are lost,
No matter what the cost
Of Government's denying,
And the only thing worse
Than beating a dead horse
Is beating one that's dying.

LIFE IS FUNNY

"Life is funny," some people say.
(But we'd be more convinced if they
Would laugh more often and be less
By envy, hate, and pride possessed.)
To many, far as I can tell,
"Life is funny" means "life is hell."

"Life is funny," we often hear
From folks who haven't smiled in years.
Job, religion, husband, or wife
Has sapped the humor from their life.
Each day dawns grayer than the last,
Because to them, "funny" means "sad."

"Life is funny," by some 'tis said.
They purse their lips and shake their head
And let us know by sighs and scowls
That they don't think it's funny at all.
To them, it seems, that "funny" stands
For "something I don't understand."

"Life is funny," others observe.
Then they go on to rant and curse
Their fate, their loved ones, and their friends.
"Funny" means "about me" to them.
But life is funny only if
You're grown up enough to laugh at it.

For humor lives outside of us
And can't survive in selfishness.
And life is funny only if we
Don't take ourselves too seriously.
"Funny" means "laughing at yourself
And giving your love to someone else."

G. E. Kruckeberg

SOME THINGS

The secret to domestic strife
Is argue with your wife.
When you're tempted to speak,
Just bite your tongue and keep your peace,
Or you'll wish you were dead.
Some things are better left unsaid.

Though business meetings are a bore,
It's not polite to snore.
And when you're asked if you
Would like to add a thing or two,
Just smile and shake your head.
Some things are better left unsaid.

When someone at a party asks
If you're a Democrat
Or one of them damn fools
That breaks the peace and bends the rules,
Ignorance should be pled.
Some things are better left unsaid.

When a car runs through a stop sign
And you hit it broadside,
If the other driver
Looks like Arnold Schwartzeneger,
Just take the blame instead.
Some things are better left unsaid.

And if your best friend's wife should ask
How much he lost at last
Night's poker game, don't stare
As if he wasn't even there.
Just say you don't recall.
Some things you never say at all.

FATCAT, PILLAGE, AND RAPE

In spite of the obvious fact that they
Were extremely, obscenely overpaid,
The team of Fatcat, Pillage, and Rape
Made Endrun Corp. what it is today.
Great team, Fatcat, Pillage, and Rape.

They say, "We made good money, it's true,
But good leadership deserves good pay."
Their leadership, though, led Endrun to
The world's greatest bankruptcy to date.
Good job, Fatcat, Pillage, and Rape!

While they told lies to the SEC
And Anderson looked the other way,
They took millions from the Company.
(How many millions no one can say –
Not even Fatcat, Pillage, and Rape.)

Before they resigned their onuses
And went their separate and merry ways,
They voted each other bonuses
And trashed their employees' 401Ks.
Thank you, Fatcat, Pillage, and Rape.

If they polluted the air and streams,
They'd probably be in jail today.
But all they destroyed were people's dreams –
While they stashed millions of dollars away.
Nice guys, Fatcat, Pillage, and Rape.

After they'd milked the Company dry,
They folded their tents and went away.
But for all the grief and misery
Somebody ought to be made to pay!
Why not Fatcat, Pillage, and Rape?

G. E. Kruckeberg

BUTTERFLIES

Life is as fragile as a butterfly,
Or as the eggs she lays (for most will die)
- As fragile as the worms that will emerge
To feed the children's cruelty – and birds,
And fragile as the chrysalis that clings
Through ice and sleet and snow to leafless limb.
But life's more wonderful, it seems to me,
Because of its innate fragility,
And though life's process wastes so much of life,
It's worth it if it makes one butterfly.

ABOUT THE AUTHOR

G. E. Kruckeberg has been an engineer, teacher, and author. He graduated from Purdue University with a Bachelor's Degree in 1962, and he studied at Sophia University in Tokyo, Japan, where he lived for six years. He has traveled extensively in the United States, Mexico, Europe, and Asia, and is now retired and living in Houston, Texas with his wife Ann, who is a writer of mystery fiction, and their three cats. This is Mr. Kruckeberg's first venture into poetry, although many of the poems in this volume are extensions of themes introduced in his earlier book, *Things My Daddy Used To Say.*

Printed in the United States
21127LVS00008B/133-135